Evolving

Devin Anna

BookLeaf Publishing

Presentation by *BookLeaf Publishing*

Web: www.bookleafpub.com

E-mail: info@bookleafpub.com

ISBN: 9789357210195

First edition 2022

DEDICATION

I dedicate this book to Colin Hassett, who was my number one supporter and friend during his time here on earth. Thank you for supporting me, my art, and my writing. I know we'll meet again someday.

The Calling

Spirit calls to me through my heart and my head
It begs and pleads for me to let it out of my heart
and into my hand
But I refuse it
Again and again

My body and mind will not work together
To let me take that chance
To let me take that risk
Of facing all the darkness
Looking at all of it
Letting it in

Because the fear of drowning
In the sorrow and grief that lives down deep
Is a threat to my ability to maintain and upkeep
All of my responsibilities

So I'm trying to heal
To reach deep down inside
To feel what is real

To find my authenticity
To find my voice and my power
To finally allow my voice to come out louder
And prouder than ever

I have no choice but to let my pen run
I have no choice but to allow these fears to come undone
Because I refuse to live in a cage that I've designed
From so much fear
That I'd ruin my own life

So with these words I'm writing now
I'm declaring that it's time
For me to stop being so afraid to write out words that rhyme
Or metaphors that climb
Into our minds

And it's time for me to allow my true rhythm to come out of hiding
To share its joy that's ever presiding
Cascading like waterfalls through the depths of my heart
These words aren't just poetry
These words are my soul's art
And to share them aloud
Outside the safety of my mind
Allows me to stand out
And finally shine

The Hidden Truth

Isn't it beautiful how the brain tries to hide
The scarier memories and moments of trauma
Deep down inside

Isn't it loving and gentle and kind
In the ways that it represses, locks away
Sometimes lies

To protect you from the truth
That could tear you apart

To pretend you have no scars
That you're an untouched work of art

Waiting to find your passion
Your purpose
Your heart

Waiting to know who you really were from the start

Your brain keeps its secrets in the most loving of ways
It keeps your darkest memories locked in a cage

Until the fateful day arrives
And the lock clicks open
Waiting for your mind
To open the door
And let the memories back inside

And it floods over you like a hose in the summer put on full blast
Like you're running through a sprinkler
But this time there are no laughs

No giggles
No hands held
No friends coming out to play

This time it's you
And your memories
However tragic
Together
They're all here to stay

As I Am

Take me as I am
Or don't take me at all

Because I'm so much more than your constructed ideas
Built by your subjective lens
Of who I once was and who you think I should be

And I will no longer be there
To catch you
When that ideal version you've created
Crumbles and shatters
And causes you to fall

Because some of that may have been me
But it was never all
All of me is incomplete
And I don't want to have to show off, earn a specific degree, show up and compete
Just to prove I'm worthy
Of being authentically me

All I need is for you to see
That who I was had hidden layers

Of who I truly wanted to be
That I was terrified would break free
Because I was worried it would never be enough

But I've had enough
I'm not playing that game anymore
Take me as I am
Scars, flaws, perceived imperfections,
Or I'll show you to the door

I don't have time to hide away anymore
I want my authentic self
The irreverent, beautiful, magical, soul she is
To take the stage
And fully have the floor

Floating

Sometimes I feel like I'm floating
Pulled by strings that seem to have no end
And throughout every bend
It seems another part of me
Has to lend
Its blame
Or even its rights
To someone else's fight

Even when I fight my own
Each and every night
The others must be always right
And I feel my chest get tight

My inner child screams
Banging and begging
Pleading
Needing
And not receiving
Any sort of validation
For the eradication
Of her innocence

Lost like a speck of dust in the lights streaming through the windows

Even the prettiest things can cause the worst
pain

But if we can learn to not run away
To look in the mirror and promise ourselves
This time I will stay
I will not turn and hide
I will not look away
You deserve to come out and play
And I will do everything in my power to validate
Myself
Creating an abundance of power
A fountain of internal wealth
A brain that no longer needs clarity around its
mental health

There is nothing more beautiful than completely
coming undone
and rebuilding yourself

The Beauty Outside

Life is beautiful if we'd only just open our eyes
It would not take something extravagant
For us to realize
There is beauty within simplicity
Within cloudy nights
And rain on the roof sounding you to sleep
There's purity in pain
And resurrection in destruction
There's truth in every lie and there's an answer to every why
But make sure that before you utter the words
You take a moment to look up at the sky
See a cloud floating by
And a bird chirping to say hi
Listen to the wind through the trees
Touch your hands to its bark
Feel its earthly energies
Let the grass grow around your feet and feel the earth and your toes meet
Let the fresh air fill your lungs
And allow the earth and your heart to become one
And that is all it will take
To realize that without this beauty
Our lives are at stake

All it will take is one more deep breath outside
One more minute spent reconnecting to nature
Allowing Mother Earth to be our most important creator
And as we spin around the equator
We will no longer find anything greater
Than the beauty that blossoms and grows around us
Surrounding us with a love so profound
All we have to do
Is simply stop to look around

Walking The Line

I don't want this apathy to keep living inside of
me
It keeps growing
Making it hard to breathe
I don't know what I see but oftentimes it seems
the truth is our deepest enemy
We walk along with the hands of time
Trying to keep our feet in line
Trying to find some peace of mind
To help us escape these trying times
But what we find is all within our mind's eye
There's no truth to be told that the infinite
knowledge of the universe doesn't already know
You carry it all within your soul
In the depths of your unconscious mind you find
ways to put your feet in line
And you move like the hands of time
Walking across the ocean shoreline
You assure yourself that someday you'll surely
find
The answer to the question of your mind
But you keep wondering why
The winds fly by and unmask your tired eyes
Telling you there's no need to hide from the
darkness inside

The most beautiful parts of life are the surface
that rests upon the dark depths
Like the blue ocean waves that roar everyday
over deeper depths than we are allowed to know
We explore the world in search of the unknown
When we all know the truth is right below
We must learn to dig deep
Finding a place farther than out of reach in order
to teach our aching hearts that our mind is a con
artist
Hoping to get some safety out of the safest
darkness
And you call yourself an artist with the hands
you use to follow time
But you can't help yourself from falling in line
Time after time
You fall back into line
Only finding yourself when you've escape your
own mind
And find the contradiction that lives between the
lines
There's no black or white just infinite shades of
grey within thin lines
Open your eyes
And your mind's eye will unwind
And tell the truth in your fear of the lack of a
construct like time
And you will remind the mind that there is an
abundance of time

Infinite and unwinding
You will keep finding
This is your time
This is your time
This is your time
Just don't fall back in line

The Persistent Fate

Have you ever had a moment
Where the universe showed that fate was real
Where it showed up on your doorstep
And changed the way you would feel
About the power of the unexpected
The make believe
The unreal
You felt it pull in your stomach
Like a knot tied tight within
A rope stretched out to the universe
And the universe grabbed the end
It told you not to listen
To those anxious voices in your head
It told you to rest your weary soul
And sleep soundly in your bed
The universe told you the things that you used to leave on read
But your mind begins to back away
When you wake up one morning
And you find those moments of synchronicity happening throughout your day
You know the power it brings you
To notice and obey
To the love that lives inside you
And pulls you through the darkest days

It's okay to lose your temper
To fight and yell and scream
But your fate will persist for you
Until you live your dreams
So take a deep breath
And relax into your human body
Life will continue in some form or another
Just take your time now
Slow down
Heal
Recover
You never know what fate has planned next
Around the corner waiting
Is a dream
A gift
A renewed sense of life
Beyond what you're anticipating

Our Internal Saviors

Is there anything more beautiful than the rawness of shame
The persistent pinch of pain that lines our eyes as we reach out a hand in a silence
To say
Here is my shame
My vulnerability and my shyness
Here are the things I'm too afraid to show the world
Or even myself

Isn't it absolutely breathtakingly beautiful, I'd show that to you and no one else?
When we feel the tap on our shoulder, begging for us to come and push our egos over
Asking us to please just give the defensiveness a rest
And we look at each other within the depths of the night time silence
When we are afraid of the walls crashing down around us
Afraid of the world pointing fingers and outing us
Trembling with the broken hearts we've been left with far too long

We grab hands and tightly hang on
Feeling each shuddering breath
As our minds and our guards slowly undress
To show each other
There is no savior more beautiful
Than our own vulnerability
Our own ability to show up with the pain that
we've refused to acknowledge for so long
To take that pain and no longer allow its control
to hold on
And use our hearts and our trusting minds
To give ourselves a glimpse of true kindness

And with a small worry this might be amiss
I lean over and whisper,
"I'm really ashamed of this"
And you watch me as I ugly cry
And tell me "darling, you and your ugly cries are
more beautiful than the combination of every
single pretty little lie"
You grab my face so gently
Caress my cheek
Beg me not to speak
With my limbs shuddering and the tears spilling
You my love, you are no villain
For there is absolutely nothing more beautiful
than this
Your shame on your lips

My hands on your hips
The love and the trust
It's electric

Not a single thing in this world of messed up
human behaviors could better exemplify what it
feels like to lose the notion that we need a savior
Because when we look into each other's eyes, on
those silent, scary nights
We find nothing but where our peace resides
Between two broken hearts knowing they will
no longer be told such nasty lies
Two women once afraid of sharing skin
So open and fearless that they hold hands and
kiss lips as they scream to each other through
closed mouths
Their shouts consisting of millions of truths that
were once shut out

You can tell me romance lies in grand gestures
Flowers and chocolates and Valentine's cards
But in my world that's a falsity so far
It makes me bleed like a piece of glass is forever
stuck in my side
It makes me want to run and hide
Because true romance exists in our pursed lips
Closing their gaps but refusing to touch as our
foreheads are the ones that kiss

So our eyes can act even more like our lips and spill our deepest secrets
That is where true love lives

Inside the secret vulnerability we once chose to hide
Inside the fist closed around a tightly grasped knife
Slowly loosening its grips
Saying "my love, I'm sorry you ever learned that knives could be used in such cruel ways"
Saying "darling, I may not be your savior, but I'll bring you to her, she's hiding behind your sad eyes"
And we look at each other with smiles
Knowing that this is real love
Sharing the scariest parts of being alive, and not having to fear if our relationship will survive
Because over and over in time
Your hand continues to find mine
Until we can unwind so easily that there is nothing shameful that cannot be spoken about freely
That is the power of vulnerability
That is the beauty of you and me

Swimming Souls

If death were a glimpse into the souls of the lost
You would think we might all stop dead in our tracks, or at the very least, pause
And give reflection in the form of affection to those who have been taught
That their long and hard years gained them millions of tears and
A family left grieving, the hope of a young child still believing,
Their dedication lost within the designation of a life no longer living
A soul is still left swimming, but who will dive in deep?
Who will take that leap? And then who will gather in awe,
To give their applause
For the sacrificial rituals we create
To begin to understand the fate
Of those who are left living without the souls they have lost

What We Long For

I remember the day it took over
Like freezing limbs in the winter cold,
I shutter and stutter as I look over my shoulder
Searching the horizon for some sign of you
To lay my eyes upon your physical body just one more time
But all I end up seeing are the tears that fall from my eyes, I still can't help but to cry
My body can't seem to let go of the words that sang the song of your passing
Bittersweet blessings and the hardest life lessons
Were all he was familiar with experiencing
No wonder he could only hear the fear
Ringing, singing, pounding
Loudly in his own head
And no, his passing was not one he was asking for
So please hold back the assumptions
Leave the harsh judgements at the door
He was pushing away a life filled with pain to try and find the surface again
Maybe he felt like he could breathe finally
After a lifetime of living in fear and suffering silently

The only voice within shouted so loud he couldn't feel anything but tears
We couldn't feel anything but tears
So he drank a poison to drown his inner voice in
Which is a problem that stems back
From a place of deep lack,
A lack of self love
That stems from a problem that a small minded perspective rests too high up above
To see its own superficial stigmatization, its own degradation of a youth lost in artificial experimentation
A lost world where people feel the need to feed the gaps within their souls
The quiet cracks and ever expanding holes
They thought their body was to always remain whole, holy, an offering,
Sacred
They masked the self hatred to the point of stripping their true selves naked
So that the depths of their pain and vulnerability are exposed
Scattered all over the floor until it finds the strength to hurt them once more
And over and over again
They sacrifice their wellbeing to the Gods of pain and misery
Just to force the voices to remain silent so that their own voice will sustain its quiet,

Timid, shy demeanor
Because you taught us that vulnerability is a weakness
And that there was no other way around it
So within the mystical substances they went diving
And deep deep down below the surface
They found it
But it wasn't the same as they'd hope for
And soon an ugly disease called addiction knocked heavily, incessantly upon their doors
And grabbed on to their minds until they became frozen in time, stuck with a one track line, repeating the words
I need it
And there was no escape as it continues to cause pain
And wreak havoc on more than just their own brains
The family and friends, they see it again and again
Attacking and attaching themselves to minds and bodies
Giving them far more than just a mouth to feed as they beg and they plead
For the one and only thing they truly need
As I've grown older, I have begun to wear their battle scars upon my own shoulders

As a commemoration to those that have loved and have lost
To those that gave everything they got, those that fought and fought
They are the souls we forgot
They are the souls some call on to rot
But I believe they are too often underestimated
They are not junkies and horrible people committing sinister acts of evil
They are running from the same pain that you feel
And their pain is just as strong, and just as real
Real enough to steal the souls of lost children
And believe me, in this case it did win
And that was the end for my brother, Colin
As he hid from the world he despised
He gained his wings to fly in a new life
And you're kidding yourself if you think I won't learn to find some new advice
Not just some new place to hide
But to find a healthier way to silence my own voices inside
Instead of reaching for a vice
I have been lucky enough to learn to think twice
And because of these lessons my family's cycle of torment has been sliced
Never again will our blood suffer inside
Our bodies will win
Our hearts will walk in stride

And I will keep moving forward, and keep fighting,
Fighting for his life
And fighting for mine

Free

I picture myself running
Dancing
Spinning
Gleefully existing
In a flowing white dress
Barefoot
Wind in my hair
Hand on my chest
Feeling my heartbeat
Along with Universe's
Wildflowers brushing past my legs
A mountain view ahead
Grassy fields under my toes
A bright blue sky overhead
A vibrant yellow sun
No one to see me
No where to be
Nothing to be done
Just me
Existing gleefully
In tune with nature
Feeling fully free

Reminders of Freedom

I hope sometimes you can find yourself lost
within that childlike innocence,
Where you feel a state of utter bliss
And the laughter roars from deep within,
stumbling out without crying for help
When the weight on your shoulders was from
your backpack on your first day of school
And not from the pain you've been harboring
and hiding from yourself
The days when you would stand up on the very
tops of your toes and reach your arms and
fingers out as far as they'd go
Grasping that forbidden item that's just out of
reach
Maybe it's toys or maybe it's hidden treats
The mountain of candy from Halloween

Back in those days, when I know you felt like a
queen
You had no reason to question your being
You lived and breathed in an air of ease
Forever at peace
With the roof over your head and the floor
beneath your feet
The love lived in the noises of the others home

The living room TV or the ringing telephone
The noises that kept you from feeling so alone

So when the night starts to call you home
And you've grown too old to be afraid of being alone
And you're too ashamed to call back home to the place that you've loathed and so long despised
Let out your cries and reach deep down inside
Underneath the pain is a child pushed aside
Left behind
Stuck at the back of the line
Reach back and offer her a soft hand
A warm embrace
Kiss her forehead and squeeze her close
Remember what it felt like to be that girl
And no longer allow her to remain a ghost
A shell of who you were
Who you wanted to be

We all have had moments that had some semblance of feeling free
So dig deeply
You will see what I mean
When I say I truly hope your childlike innocence can come out to play
To show you the brightness on the darkest of days

To take you away to an imaginary land of
make-believes and fairy tales
Where laughter abounds
And dancing and running is always allowed
Where yelling with joy shows the world that
you're proud

I hope you find that sound
Within yourself, I hope you find this all out
And stop that self doubt
Learning to let the bad voices out
You no longer have to shout for your acceptance
Embrace the innocence
Embrace the chances
The changes
Let the laughter be contagious
And be so silly it's outrageous
We all need a chance to start again
So let yourself out
Revel in her goofy beautiful dance

The Light Wins

The day you left I could still so vividly hear
your voice bouncing around my head
The thought of you continues to be an echoed
shout that never ends
I want to scream some days, let loose, let the bad
times in,
I want to give up sometimes and let those bad
times win
But these days I must remember to pat my own
back
And remind myself that what you did, while it
may have been unintentional,
What you did changed the world
And as I try not to let the guilt consume my soul
I remember that you too had goals,
And you too had demons that wore down your
soul
And that golden light that you shine for me, the
one displaying the truest parts of your beauty
Lives on, stronger, brighter, and more apparent
than ever
Because the pain that you carried for 22 years,
please know
I carried it too
The trauma you faced,

The addictions you dealt with,
The guilt you felt,
The loneliness,
The fear,
And the wonder,
I felt it too
I saw it too
And I knew it just as well
This is why we were always so close,
Brother and sister,
Best friends until the end
Well I am here as living, breathing proof,
That what was once started must commence until its own end
And your friendship and strength
Must double in space
And I must allow that in
So in an effort to honor you,
Remember your goals,
And to make them come true,
I must choose not let those demons win
I was always too afraid of what would happen anyway,
If I'd followed our parents examples, and let the poison help them swim
Who knows if I'd ever have the strength to beat the demons again
And I know you worried this too,
But for you, there wasn't enough time to choose

By the time the drugs stole your human consciousness
Your soul was already shedding its demons off
And lighting up the world from a higher dimension
And as the pain taps against my gut,
Rhythmically I hear that echoed voice again
I hear your name, and beg for your face
In this humanistic place
Just one more day
So I can show you, that the universe took the bad away
And it made you whole again
And those demons, even if you cannot see it
They did not win

A Story Untold

Learn what it means to truly let go
Explore the wild, reckless abandon that is your soul
And soon enough a story will unfold
Where Earth will share her secrets,
Her treasures,
Her gold
With those few so brave enough
To ignore what they've been told
Who step outside of their comforts to discover
The story that is yet to be told
Of the magic that exists
Within and without
Of our minds, bodies, and souls

Earth's Peace

Sometimes it seems there is so much human
noise
An abundance of grown up little boys
With their big, industrial toys
Automatic, rapturing
Tossing,
Turning
It can be so loud that you no longer hear a small
bird sing
Over the sound of a careless human with trash to
fling
An ocean overflowing with our waste
It is no longer a metaphor
It is proof most have been raised
To embellish in poor taste
And I cover my ears and turn away my face
Trying to hide from the destruction
Of such a magical place
It is so hard to belong to a species that believes
Their existence is the most important of all time
and space
Quite frankly, it is a disgrace
Something that feels impossible to escape
But I am here to save Earth's fate
So no matter how hard it is for me

To sit by a tree and find distraction among all the noise of machines
Earth needs me
At the base of each tree
Grounding, growing, rooting
Into her rich soils
Sending love where they are out stealing oils
So I lean my head against a tree
I practice meditating, envisioning an Earth so free
That the sound of life in all of its forms
Splashes against all of these human shores
And makes our toes freeze,
Stops our motions
Forcing us to listen to the sounds of the ocean
This is unfiltered nature,
Earth's poetry
Singing beautifully,
In motion

Choose Your Path

You define your life
You and only you

You can create your destiny
Your path is yours alone to choose

Sometimes it may seem hard
Some days you'll want to give up the fight

But soon you'll open up your eyes
To once again greet the morning light

And somewhere along the journey
You'll stop to look at the sky
And realize that dreams were never meant
To be just clouds of thought floating by

You'll reach out a hand and touch something
So physical, so tangible, so real
And you'll know in your heart for the first time
ever
That your wishes were granted
Your thoughts were enchanted
And your magic most certainly had the power to
reveal

A life path aligned with your most abundant ideals

Treehouse

I want to live in a tree house
High up in the clouds
I want to live in a treehouse
Far away from everyone else
I want to spend my days
Resting
Healing
Recovering
Feeling
High up in the clouds
I want to live in a tree house
To gain a perspective from above
I want to live in a treehouse
To feel the heavenly love
To see the birds flying by
And to feel the breeze in the sky
I want to live in a tree house
High up in the clouds

Glowing

Like a needle pulling a string
From my heart to the back of my chest
It is a rope playing tug of war
It feels like a fatal conquest
From my heart to the new door
I used to beg the universe
I begged and pleaded for more
For some new pathway
A glowing light under an opening door
But my heart sank when I saw one
Because I didn't trust it
But this is a conquest I will complete
I will not allow fear to stop me
I truly won't
I will wear my heart on my sleeve
Be as open to the world as I please
Because telling the truth is a must
And soon enough, afterwards,
I'll know who I can trust
I'll follow the path as I must
And within the universe I will return my worries
to dust
Starting anew along the rightly glowing path
The right path
With the right me

Your Soundscape

The soundscape of my life plays
Like a portrait of your face on repeat
In the back of my mind
Giving me no freedom from the confines
Of the world within these lines
I gasp for a breath of frozen air
And I swallow the taste of pine
I wonder if everyone has a similar relationship with time
A never ending struggle to unwind
The power cords that dictate your mind
But your mind's eye can't seem to find that light to trace
Wandering at a slow yet unsteady pace
The only solace to be found
Is when I trace the imaginary soundscape of your life
All the way back to the sharpest knife
The knife that sliced right through all of our lives
We never knew we could be content
No longer asking why
But if I had just listened
To each heartbeat gone by
Maybe I would find that time

And you and I would meet again
As we listened to our Dad's songs
We'd sit back
And truly learn what it means to just unwind
Finally experiencing the joy of having an
innocently good time
No more faded lines and crushed minds
No more experimental substances for you to try
No more fear and no more tears
No more worries to combine
The two of us have it figured out this time
Maybe then the soundscape will portray a new
version
Of you and I
Where we are flying high off of the sustenance
Of the earth and the sky
Where nothing more is left
To be desired

www.ingramcontent.com/pod-product-compliance
Lightning Source LLC
Chambersburg PA
CBHW051744130826
49812CB00033B/992
9789357210195